THE HOLY & BROKEN BLISS

B

POEMS IN PLAGUE TIM

ALICE JAMES BOOKS
New Gloucester, ME
alicejamesbooks.org

THE HOLY & BROKEN BLISS

ALICIA OSTRIKER

10 9 8 7 6 5 4 3 2 1

Alice James Books are published by Alice James Poetry Cooperative, Inc.

Alice James Books
Auburn Hall
60 Pineland Drive, Suite 206
New Gloucester, ME 04260
www.alicejamesbooks.org

Library of Congress Cataloging-in-Publication Data

Names: Ostriker, Alicia, author.
Title: The holy & broken bliss : poems in plague time / Alicia Ostriker.
Other titles: The holy and bliss
Description: New Gloucester, ME : Alice James Books, 2024.
Identifiers: LCCN 2024020532 (print) | LCCN 2024020533 (ebook)
   ISBN 9781949944679 (trade paperback) | ISBN 9781949944396 (epub)
Subjects: LCGFT: Poetry.
Classification: LCC PS3565.S84 H65 2024 (print) | LCC PS3565.S84 (ebook)
   | DDC 811/.54--dc23/eng/20240510
LC record available at https://lccn.loc.gov/2024020532
LC ebook record available at https://lccn.loc.gov/2024020533

Alice James Books gratefully acknowledges support from individual donors,
private foundations, the National Endowment for the Arts, and the Poetry
Foundation (https://www.poetryfoundation.org).

Cover Art: © 2023 The Willem de Kooning Foundation / Artists Rights
Society (ARS), New York. Digital image © Whitney Museum of American Art /
Licensed by Scala / Art Resource, NY

CONTENTS

THESE BE THE WORDS . . .

ONE
I CANNOT DO THIS IN PROSE | 3
TIME | 4
SLOWLY | 5
SLOWLY | 6
WE ALL KNOW | 7
WHAT THEY SAY, SLOWLY THEY SAY, THEY SAY | 8

TWO
TIME | 13
PLAGUE TIME RITUAL I | 14
PLAGUE TIME RITUAL II | 15
SUMMER | 16
EVENING IN PLAGUE TIME | 18
DEMONSTRATION IN PLAGUE TIME | 19

THREE
HAIKU | 23
DOUBLE PLAGUE | 24
ALL THAT YEAR | 25
ELUL | 26
AT THE CENTER | 28
TACHYCARDIA | 29

FOUR

FEVER | 33

THE SALLEY GARDENS | 34

THE HIGH BOARD | 35

HELPMATE | 36

BEAUTY (A DROP OF DOPAMINE) | 37

BREAKFAST | 38

FEEDING BREADCRUMBS TO BIRDS | 39

FIVE

TIME | 43

LATE AUTUMN GINKGOS | 44

KEEPING THE DRAGON | 45

ORACLE: IN THE OLD DAYS | 46

ORACLE: AFTER | 47

THE PARABLE OF THE UMBRELLA THORN TREE | 48

NOCTURNE | 50

ANYTHING IN MOTION | 52

GOLDBERG VARIATIONS IN DOUBLE-PLAGUE TIME | 53

PRAYER | 54

SIX

LATE WINTER IN PLAGUE TIME | 57

SOLITUDE | 58

WHEN WE WAKE IN THE MORNING | 59

TACHYCARDIA (AGAIN) | 60

MOTHER/DAUGHTER DREAM | 61

PHOTO OF A YOUNG WOMAN | 62

THE MIND SECEDES | 63

THE OLD WOMAN READS ECCLESIASTES AND THE SONG
    OF SONGS | 64

SEVEN

PRAYER TO THE SHEKHINAH | 69

THE REPLY | 70

SPEAKING SLOWLY, SOFTLY, SHE SAYS | 71

CONFESSION: WHEN I CHOSE HIM | 72

OSTINATO | 73

SOME NIGHTS | 74

THE WINGS OF THE SHEKHINAH (THIS ONE AFTERNOON
     WHILE I WORK AT MY DESK) | 75

THE CHANNEL, THE PIPE, SHE SAYS, THEY SAY | 77

THE FORCE THAT SENDS LIGHT | 78

CODA | 79

AFTER/WORD | 81

ACKNOWLEDGMENTS | 87

The peach petals would like to stay,
But moon and wind blow them on.
        —Hanshan, translated by A.S. Kline

        In *The Penguin Book of Spiritual Verse*, ed. Kaveh Akbar

THESE BE THE WORDS...

—Deuteronomy 1, KJV

The words of an old woman shuffling the cards of her own
    decline   the decline
of her husband   the decline of her nation   her plague-smitten
    world

virus that has slain its millions   rage and despair driving the
    body politic
into violent writhings   knotted upheavings   drama I watch
    from the wings

telling myself: These too are the wings of the Shekhinah
    beneath which I arise
and shower   dress in the morning   undress at night   in my
    house of many doors

many windows little sky
song reversed to clanging   alarm   alarm

Write if you can find words I tell myself   write what you are
    afraid to write
lay down your cards   step over the lintel through that door:
    Write or die.

ONE

I CANNOT DO THIS IN PROSE

Words gone
back where they came from

it is not a joke
what is lost will not return

it will not happen all at once
but it will happen

it will happen over time

TIME

Time is like a twisted arm

my husband is sleeping more hours

walking much more slowly

SLOWLY

He goes down

the stone steps

from the apartment building

to Riverside Park

holding the rail   holding his balance

the summer vegetation riots and rots

around his sandaled feet

SLOWLY

The image of a man

walking slowly down a set of stone stairs

recurs in my dreams

has recurred in my dreams

for fifty years

what it means

we all know

WE ALL KNOW

The hour of our death
the meaning of our life

what will happen afterward
exactly where we go

the monsters we then will encounter
the joy-embracing gods

the dust

WHAT THEY SAY, SLOWLY THEY SAY, THEY SAY

It is not a bridge
it is a rejoining
they say

they say
it is a rejoining
not a bridge

not a bridge to imagined
torments or cloudlets
but the slow return

of our being to you
back along the path where we began
returning to you

like a child
tired of freedom
needing the smell of the mother

they say that

*

the tipping point of this life
streaming back
to you

they say

TWO

TIME

Time goes by
day trailing day
it passes me by
and somehow fades
like a stealthy black cat
like an old scar
like a recently cleaned
express subway car
lit up boldly inside there it goes
loudly clacking
gradually passing
the local subway car
covered with graffiti
in which I sit sighing
watching golden-windowed Time slide by
both trains move
one moves faster
wait up
no

PLAGUE TIME RITUAL I

We no longer leave the apartment   we cook
or order in and eat amply together

I make a pleasing borscht   he a pleasing French
onion soup   together we dance

the long-married kitchen dance
he is slowly steadily losing weight

he jokes that he will not die
he will grow smaller and smaller

until I can carry him around in a teacup
exhibit him to my friends

PLAGUE TIME RITUAL II

As I daily wipe
each piece of mail
with Clorox
before opening
to protect myself from the virus
I wish I could wipe myself clean
of envy
of anger
symptoms of another lifelong
contagious illness

I don't believe in original sin
so what in hell
is it
infecting me year after year
traveling through space
in bullets of resentment
greed   terror   blood
wounded
how cleanse
how heal

SUMMER

It is summer still   hot sun
trees heavy with foliage

loud birds in the shrubbery
hiding from hawks

neglected towers collapsing
and the plagues of poverty

and addiction and despair
and the attack of the invisible

against a temple here or there
white stone   gone dead

What am I to make of all this beauty
and all this sorrow

please just act like normal
like everything will be okay

please trust the system
say the system managers

from nowhere a woman   nameless
stands up   shouting

watch out for the angels
they despise you

there they go flying over you
heading for the coast

coughing garbage
into the atmosphere

above you

EVENING IN PLAGUE TIME

We hand ourselves over to the media
the media hands us over to profit

    we are not what we were
    we will not be what we are

we are possessed
we no longer even yell
at the news

DEMONSTRATION IN PLAGUE TIME

They call their region the flyover states
states of trash   cockroaches   despisals

today they are demonstrating against vaccination
It's all about anger, isn't it   anger   and hurt beneath it

the disrespect   the disrespect hurts like anything
halo of piquant mosquitos humming

they are dying of the rank disrespect
dying of disease   drink and drugs   suicide

If anyone has arms long enough
to reach past the anger to embrace the hurt

that alligator in your belly that repetitive mockery
if the magic of love exists

anywhere, let us imagine a superhero president
pulling it out of his sleeve   a rainbow scarf   a mitten

from the cedar chest of a painful childhood   they say
that is what Jesus did   simply reached out to the hurt

with arms like tree boughs
fingers like springtime petals

THREE

HAIKU

In one sorry blink
the black man killed by the cop
fills the white pavement

DOUBLE PLAGUE

Thanks to the virus
every breath we breathe we risk
inhaling a death

and the other plague
continues tweeting its hate
oiling the weapons

ALL THAT YEAR

For Cynthia Hogue

We were bodysurfing a wave of public venom
attempting to swim   it was terrific   thrilling
hate sprayed us on the left and on the right
we wondered   would it smash us into a reef

on-screen our swaggering leader   man we elected
loosed lies from his lips like eels
it was a good moment for cartoonists and journalists
and billionaires and lovers of guns   a good moment

for poets   poets thrive on disaster
born as we are within the wound

ELUL

I am climbing a wet, slippery rock face
I have no gear
can't see to the top or the bottom

looking around I observe many
other climbers
clinging to the same wet rock

I was standing at the shallow end of a wading pool
splashing like a kindergartener   and now
I enjoy watching my quiet pink feet

against the turquoise and pearly pebbly concrete
of the pool floor how strange
how strange old age

has brought me here

*

I greet the trees in the park
they return my greeting
courteously
I say to my husband
I am convinced the trees are sentient beings
he replies
I bet they make the same mistake about you

*

Ovid knew
trees are people

demons live in oaks
at midnight sycamores strip

*

When we pray
to the sefirot of the trees
the trees inquire
Can we pray
for the hidden women of Afghanistan
for the rubble-housed children of Haiti
for the boys in brilliant sneakers shooting each other
in the morning news
and for the murdered journalists here and there

*

Now that the sycamores
are losing their leathery leaves
now that the rain forests are up in smoke
like the drinkers of black milk in Poland
now that I still cannot divest myself
of anger and envy
my personal sins

whose is the voice demanding I choose life

AT THE CENTER

At the center for disease control
they are not slackers
they work like beavers
Science   the hero
fights the virus   the virus
ducks and weaves

the dying keep trying to breathe
the bereaved surrender in tears
Mama Gaia remains unappeased
walking up and down on earth
we have all insulted her
she will have her revenge

Yes   that is how she thinks
you better beware a woman
a mother   wronged   humiliated
better believe she will do anything
within her power
to retaliate

What if she too considers suicide

TACHYCARDIA

Tachycardia all day yesterday
faint 8 a.m.
by evening a fast thud-thud
insistent as if someone is trying
to tell me something
in a language I don't know
the sign language
of an entity
that expresses itself in rhythm
and is becoming impatient
with my ignorance
we used to understand each other
perfectly
or so I thought
I thought we were like sisters

now it seems for eighty years
she has labored nonstop
thump thump 24/7
without complaint
I have been like some plantation mistress
believing in my own benevolence
believing I and my personal
house slave
understand each other
now my heart is racing

as if to get away
through the underground
to freedom

FOUR

FEVER

Those days when he was feverish
and could do nothing but sleep
those days when I said please
drink something   eat somethIng
and he refused
Those days were a little...
a little rehearsal

THE SALLEY GARDENS

She bid me take life easy
As the grass grows on the weirs
But I was young and foolish
And now am full of tears
    —W.B. Yeats

We listen to the Celtic station
while we exercise
today they are playing
that beautiful Yeats song
Down by the Salley Gardens again
he pauses in his push-ups
he says he doesn't care how
often they play it
he still loves it   his eyes are wet
as the grass   I like that
blur

THE HIGH BOARD

Every night
he dives backward off the high board
of the day
entering without a splash
the world of his early childhood
that smells like oranges
and butter
where his mother and grandmothers
play with him and teach him things
when I try to waken him
he resists he
clings to that world

HELPMATE

In my dream
when I murmur
I won't be able
to live without you
he gallantly replies
yes you will
In real life he would say
he worries about me

Who will fix my computer
when it goes on strike again
and I panic   who will do
the complicated
financial logistics
who will stop me
from carelessly setting
the house on fire

BEAUTY (A DROP OF DOPAMINE)

Just now
while I was at the sink
drying dishes
they caught my eye
those orange
Peruvian
lilies on
the table with the old
Iranian tablecloth
at other times it is
his aging sculpted face
or his hands
at rest on a book
while he naps

BREAKFAST

If I say *tart, crisp*
have I stated all that need be stated
about the apple?

Should I append the cheddar cheese
aged three or is it seven years
that combines so well with the apple?

Should the context include
the conversation with my husband
about the shooter

whose mother had called him
mentally ill   and whose father
had given him the gun?

Or the numbers on
the virus this morning? What
the charts show

of deaths in each state
and city and neighborhood
compared with

yesterday or last
week? What
happens to the apple then?

FEEDING BREADCRUMBS TO BIRDS

Feeding breadcrumbs to birds
    we laugh at how the sparrows
surge and dart past the beaks
    of the slow pigeons

FIVE

TIME

Time is but the stream I go a-fishing in
remarks Thoreau   implying that he himself is immortal

or perhaps that the stream of time is the piss of god
an indelicate way to put it   and yet   the pure transparency…

To me it is a nerve   slicing unruffled
 between cold fleshy banks   half paralyzed I feel

like an owl watching the stars revolve
looking like tiny lit-up mice

To itself the stream I name *time* is possibly yearning   struggling
        full of
helpless fear and submission   cut through the material world
        a being

racing toward ocean hoping to be clean   fertile   awash in fish
for Henry David Thoreau   and Elizabeth Bishop   to catch
            and release

and then to be lost and gone
no more identity   no further fear

LATE AUTUMN GINKGOS

Sunlight revels through ginkgos
   alongside Broadway traffic
      radiance attacks the season
         ecstatic yellow shining

It is almost winter and still
   as I walk to the clinic the gingkos
      sing their seraphic air
         as if there is no tomorrow

They learned it back in the Permian
   before the belated ferns
      the flowery deciduous
         and the needled coniferous

cousins arrived on earth
   bringing alto tenor and bass lines
      to the long soprano arpeggio
         we latecomers overhear
         half deaf though we be

KEEPING THE DRAGON

A woman who looks like Gertrude Stein
in the Picasso portrait
sits in my armchair and speaks:

We have slain the many gods
they were unreal
the one god in whom we say we believe
is also unbelievable
humanism keeps the dragon
as a kind of toy
no
as a mask

ORACLE: IN THE OLD DAYS

They always knew about death
they needed to decide what to do about it

some decided to deny it was real
some invented dances

some stayed angry
some killed their own sons

ORACLE: AFTER

The beings after the Anthropocene
will be formed of inorganic matter
they will be not unfeeling
they will study us
the way we study the natural world
they will have libraries   zoos
stocked with us

the ones after them
will be made of cloud

THE PARABLE OF THE UMBRELLA THORN TREE

after Peter Wohlleben, The Hidden Life of Trees

The story says
when the giraffes started to eat
the leaves of the umbrella thorn tree
the trees did not like it one bit
and rapidly pumped some home-grown
poison into their leaves
causing the giraffes to flee

The author of this story
with his anthropomorphizing mind
and casual colloquial style
means us to understand that trees
have purpose, pleasure,
and power
at their leaftips

Lucky for us they can't uproot themselves
and come after us   we genocidal maniacs
who have murdered trillions
of their kin   vengeance
the strangling grip in every root
the choking sap in every twig   they would win
because they are older and wiser

We would lose because we are younger
and stupider   so something must be done
and if I were president I would mandate
tree planting quotas for all citizens
all families   all teenagers   all university students
and professors   all bankers and corporate
executives   more trees   more trees
an ecological turning point

What is a turning point?   Rosa making a speech in a bus
Johnson getting the voting bill past the Senate then
remarking *There goes the South.*   There's a worm
that's turning and turning two ways at once   tying itself
into a not   But my mom thought Education
was the answer   my dad thought Down with the bosses
Up with the working classes   and Emily said

what she said about Hope   Maybe Emily was sitting
under an umbrella thorn tree
where the aggressive giraffes couldn't get her.

NOCTURNE

A man sleeps in his car
in the fast food parking lot
a cop knocks on his window

the man is passive as a peony
gets out of the car   hands over
his papers without complaint

does the Breathalyzer quietly then
the cop leans over the man's ear
begins to arrest him

parking lot lights cast a cindery gleam
on the naked speckled asphalt
the video camera stares

suddenly the man fights
like a tiger   struggles free   runs
is shot   dies   we wonder

was it the handcuffs
drove the man mad like that
or something else

can we guess what word
the cop whispered
in that black man's ear

that night

ANYTHING IN MOTION

A small girl in the park runs ahead of her mother
skipping   jumping and giggling
looking back over her shoulder
to make sure the mother is still there
because what   if she is gone

I like seeing her do this   the mother likes it
it makes the mother smile
the older brother also smiles
because he loves her   I surmise
he is a sweet boy who truly loves her

the sky above the park parades some clouds
the family heads for the row of swings
I try to imagine them painted by Monet
in one of his pastoral scenes
but Monet does not paint anything in motion

happiness needs to express itself in motion
I don't have my camera with me
what I have is my eyes   my need to praise

GOLDBERG VARIATIONS IN DOUBLE-PLAGUE TIME

Bach on an odd traditional instrument   half lute
half keyboard   streams at me from my small
wide screen   These famous frolics this epic banter
composed in an age of science   an age of enlightenment

arrives in a time of disastrous pandemic   coupled with tribal
malignancy and violence   to which it offers the charming
remedy of variation: The horizon blown in the wind
will always recede   the grooved pattern will always vary

The piece is being performed by a handsome Chinese youth
in a Regency sitting room   the chair seats are burgundy velvet
and it takes perhaps twenty minutes to perform the quick and
     slow
the gorgeous   the elaborate   the ingenious variations

Curled on my living room sofa I listen and imagine
this music performed in the home of an opulent Hapsburg
     burgher
whose perfumed wife has composed the guest list
and whose perfumed guests are not permitted to be restless

The ghost of Bach in my living room requests
that my husband and I also be quiet and pay attention
Now too everything changes and remains the same
Listen   now too in glory the world revolves

PRAYER

For Raya on her bat mitzvah

The force that sends light
through the cracks
in everything
needs eyes   to see

May it find you
may it find your eyes
enlighten your mind
gladden your days

May your eyes see the beauty
and sorrow of the world
clearly and keenly   oh
and may light lead you to love

SIX

LATE WINTER IN PLAGUE TIME

We permit ourselves
a walk every day
we believe outdoors is safe
we remove our masks
and the trees in Riverside Park
are so individual
the curved or abrupt
swerves of their boughs appear
to demonstrate free will
in cahoots with biology so
then one day
crossing the street to the park
something in the air   not wind
not fragrance
brushes against my body
surges like breakers
from the row of leafless sycamores
what can it be
it must be the sap rising   yes
today must be the day the sap
begins to rise
exciting the trees so that
their bodies emit waves of a chemical
science cannot yet name
which my own body
can sense
even in the midst of winter
even in the midst of plague

SOLITUDE

I am at my desk in the late afternoon
earlier I was napping   there was rain
he came in to tell me there was rain
he needed to wake me up to tell me

I said I was sleeping   and was in the mood
for solitude   the idea startled him

After the rain down in the back courtyard
I was sitting at my desk listening
to the sound of bottles being loaded
into transparent plastic garbage bags

WHEN WE WAKE IN THE MORNING

I bury my nose in his neck and breathe it in

TACHYCARDIA (AGAIN)

Either I forgot
my pills last night or
mother is knocking
from the other world
desperate to get
inside me again
the way she used to
when she was alive
and I would let her
twist around my heart
and keep on talking

Possibly the moment has come
to open the shutters
and let the woman in
with her swanlike honking
her mad cow
possessiveness and her
high hopes
for her daughter

(So many times observing
the laptop screen afire
with my guilty love
I have said
this is the last poem
I will write
about my mother)

MOTHER / DAUGHTER DREAM

My dream shrinks to a dot
it goes where my mother went
unwillingly

I remember that there is really no death
she might come back
crazier than before

or she might come back healed
the fight gone out of her

PHOTO OF A YOUNG WOMAN

A young woman in a chair
pressing herself
into her son
I was   that young woman

who adores that baby
whose breasts sing
hymns to that baby
about whom she is utterly ignorant

and when we   were lovers
pressing into each other
mouth   to mouth
like God and Moses

didn't our young bodies press
and
sing very much like that

.

THE MIND SECEDES

For Rebecca Gayle Howell

The mind walks the dog
around the block
as usual

but coming back
finds
nobody home

the mind then cannot help
but notice its own
gradual

withdrawal   its
white
erasure

knowing
his body will go
her mind will

THE OLD WOMAN READS ECCLESIASTES AND THE SONG OF SONGS

—*Ecclesiastes 12.1,6; Song of Songs 2.16*

Before
      before the evil days come
            when I will say I have no pleasure
in them   and
before
      the golden bowl owl old
           old   old   old
           woman they say

*

be broken

*

the wheel broken at
my beloved is mine

I have two tasks
and I am his

Find truer language for the plague year   the bardo year
(very like the Holland Tunnel endless gray)

Take my bulletproof vest   off, take it off

I mean I wish

I mean I need to love   with the love   that is like milk   before
the pitcher shatters

finally I did so with my mother   love   flawed   flowed
I do it in moments   with my man   down the mountain we go

over the crumbling ice   gripping hard earth
not running   careful not to trip

over a root or a rock
and fall and break

a leg bone   or skull
down the mountain we

go   go slowly
limping slightly

fighting the fight in us   old
eruptions of anger envy pride

or bliss singing the song in us
they say is stronger than death

smoke help me
wine help me

Shekhinah help me
to love without cause without cease

help me believe
existence itself bliss

broken and we
alone required to mend it

SEVEN

PRAYER TO THE SHEKHINAH

In my prayers night and day
is the hope that you will visit me
which possibly you have been doing
all the while inside my skin
producing hymnodies of birth   of lamentation
lifted from every mass grave in the world
scratching me   pinching me from inside
calling me an idiot
since I do not know how to reach you
by myself in the carapace of this body
struggling like the turtle
to move as fast as I can
and not get run over crossing the street

you at a distance beloved my mother my daughter
you at a distance my soul who remains at a distance
they say you will travel to meet me
if I travel to meet you   pity I am so slow
but am grateful for the handful of past
moments you have spoken with me   the fool
who hoped to be counted among the poets
weeping along the path to her own soul

THE REPLY

Walking slowly down stone steps
into a basement

the damp smell
the darkness

things strewn around
broken   rusty

don't turn back
find the light switch

find the channel   the pipe   find
water rushing through blackness

SPEAKING SLOWLY, SOFTLY, SHE SAYS

Pay attention my dear
not long from now   not far from here
like many of your elderly friends
aching with their struggles
you will embark
on the medical mystery tour
through a peninsula of loss

When you enter at length
the cave of quiet time
among the rocks the mossy walls
the families of bats   so much depends
upon chance in the form
of the nurse currently on call
hopefully one of my granddaughters

who will take your trembling hand
and lead you
through its polished marble labyrinths
by the rhythms of your body's decline
the drumtaps pacing the flute
down to the river
that flows through blackness

bangles agleam on her wrist
get in the boat she will say
reaching out her hand to help

CONFESSION: WHEN I CHOSE HIM

He was the one
the quintessence of energy
of energy and wit

sweetie I say stop making me laugh
when I laugh (at my age) I have to pee
and you know my bladder

is like a talkative old person
when they pause you may think they are done
but not at all

and there was always
the river rushing through blackness
inside him

OSTINATO

He was the one
the unpredictable   hairy
monkey among the puppets

cheerful contrarian
perfecting his serve
and his equations

and there was always
the river rushing through blackness
guiding him

SOME NIGHTS

Before we fall asleep
he asks me to recite
Prospero's our revels
now are ended speech
for I am his designated
Shakespeare consultant
other nights he reads
Dickens to me
or Isaac Bashevis Singer
or David Hume
or Laozi
while the light   the light
of one billion high-redshift
galaxies drives
past our verdant planet
and our cream-white
bedroom walls
curving and
curving

THE WINGS OF THE SHEKHINAH (THIS ONE AFTERNOON WHILE I WORK AT MY DESK)

She is standing there
at my painted door

whenever I glance over she seems
at ease   unagitated   patient

she looks back at me
affectionately smiling

the way grown-ups smile
at a child learning to walk

or aim a spoon at its mouth
or hold a crayon

*

Years ago at times
while trying to meditate
or to improve a poem I sensed
a trio of young women who seemed
to belong to the spirit world
standing behind my chair
or behind me on the grass
giggling a little
I guessed they were her daughters

I never saw them but I knew
they were there
gently laughing at me

*

the dress she wears is green
and loose   her hair is white

her wings are invisible
like my wound

THE CHANNEL, THE PIPE, SHE SAYS, THEY SAY

The water rushing through darkness   the spark
rushing through darkness   go ahead

dive on in   beloved

they say   there are as many neurons in your head
as galaxies in the universe

breathe in the aroma of the cave

the water rushing through darkness   the spark
floating through darkness   go ahead

dive in with the discarded things   beloved
breathe in the aroma of the cave

they say   there are more neurons in your head
than stars in the milky way   go ahead   dive in

THE FORCE THAT SENDS LIGHT

May it find me
may it find my eyes
illuminate my mind
gladden my waning days

may the One who writes
in the book of life
inscribe my name
among the poets

may I learn to read it
may my humble
request for more light
more time be honored

CODA

Let my poems be shards of the holy and broken bliss
that circles and shackles the earth

AFTER/WORD

Most of the poems in this collection arrived during the years 2020–22, that is to say the plague years. I had not planned for them but was intensely grateful as I, like so many others, was living through this sick period in a sort of exhausted limbo or bardo state of immobility.

THESE BE THE WORDS . . . : In the King James translation, *These be the words which Moses spake unto all Israel on this side Jordan in the wilderness.* That is, where they could see the promised land but could not yet enter it. Moses himself was prevented from ever entering it. Aaron and Miriam never even came close. It was the young warrior Joshua who crossed over into the land. It was Joshua who took over. Joshua who shaped the future of Israel as a future of almost continual warfare.

The wings of the Shekhinah: The Shekhinah in Kabbalah is the feminine half of God's identity sundered from its masculine half at the moment of creation. He is the divine Transcendence. She is the divine Presence. She is the energy immanent in every atom of the material world. We are protected by her wings. At the end of time the broken pair will be reunited and their name will be One. Jewish husbands and wives make love on the eve of the Sabbath in order to model that reunion.

Write or die: The poet H.D. as an old woman tells herself this in her last book, *Hermetic Definition.*

SLOWLY: *The image of a man / walking slowly down a set of stone stairs:* William Blake's etching of an old man entering a cavelike door made of huge hewn stones is unforgettable.

WE ALL KNOW: How do we "know" anything? With what conscious or unconscious mechanism of our brains do we "know" things? How is it that we can know things without being aware that we do? Is there a dimension outside of time in which all is known?

SUMMER: *Neglected towers collapsing:* The collapse of a badly built residential high-rise in London, Ont., December 11, 2020, was the story of the week for a week. Other collapses of tall buildings reported that year included the Arecibo Observatory in Puerto Rico and the Juxian Restaurant in Shanxi, China. Buildings collapse throughout the world every year. I am reminded of T.S. Eliot's "Unreal cities" and his litany of "Falling towers / Jerusalem Athens Alexandria / Vienna London / Unreal." The paradoxes of capitalism.

A woman   nameless: The Cassandra-like woman is the first of several named and nameless females making an appearance in these poems. I do not know their origin but suspect them to be avatars of the Shekhinah. I believe Gaia is one of her daughters. They arrive riding the wind that blows through me.

Watch out for the angels: These would be Blake's pious self-satisfied angels in *The Marriage of Heaven & Hell.* They are also Boeing 747s.

DEMONSTRATION IN PLAGUE TIME: *cockroaches   despisals:* See and hear Muriel Rukeyser, "St. Roach" and "Despisals," both available online.

ALL THAT YEAR: The year is 2021, a year that will live in the annals of what the Chinese call "interesting times." Similar in a way to 1968.

ELUL: The month in the Jewish calendar in which we take stock of our lives, preparing ourselves for the High Holidays in which we attempt to return to God.

The drinkers of black milk in Poland: See Paul Celan, "Todesfugue," available online in several translations.

TACHYCARDIA: The heart races. It is not a fatal condition but it is disruptive.

TIME: *Time is but the stream:* a famous sentence in Thoreau's *Walden.* The full passage can be found online.

THE PARABLE OF THE UMBRELLA THORN TREE: *and Emily [Dickinson] said / what she said about Hope:* that it was a thing with feathers; find the poem online.

MOTHER/DAUGHTER DREAM: *there is really no death:* Walt Whitman, "Song of Myself." *The smallest sprout shows there is really no death . . . . / All goes onward and outward, nothing collapses, / And to die is different from what any one supposed, and luckier.* The entire poem is available online.

PHOTO OF A YOUNG WOMAN: *like God and Moses:* God declares of Moses, *with him will I speak mouth to mouth, even manifestly, and not in dark speeches;* that is, not in riddles or mystifications. Numbers 12.8, available online. The divine kiss is what all seekers seek.

THE OLD WOMAN READS ECCLESIASTES AND THE SONG OF SONGS: Can we choose the time of our death? Can we quit while we are ahead? The soul-advice suggesting we make the most of life *Before the evil days come and the years draw near when you shall say I have no pleasure in them* is Ecclesiastes 12.1. My mother did not read Ecclesiastes, but she said the same, that she hoped to die when life stopped being enjoyable. *My beloved is mine and I am his* is the Song of Songs 2.16. Death and love our pinnacles of achievement. The awakening of mind framed by death and love.

The bardo year: The bardo in various Eastern traditions is a transitional state between death and rebirth, a state of blank nothingness in some branches, of testing in others, of meeting and resisting/ overcoming the temptations and monsters of life in the material world. By common agreement, the bardo exists between our death and our rebirth. I felt myself to be living in the bardo during the period of the plague. There was no air. I could not write. For a year and a half I could not write. When the words began to come, I was reborn. Alive again, like others.

PRAYER TO THE SHEKHINAH: that you will visit me: as Jesus visited St. Paul and numerous medieval nuns, Krishna visited Radha, the cowherd girls, and the poet Mirabai, God the Father visited the Beguine Mechtilde of Magdeburg, Milton visited Blake, and the Lady in "Tribute to the Angels" visited H.D.

THE CHANNEL, THE PIPE, SHE SAYS, THEY SAY: *Dive on in, beloved . . .* I cannot now remember where I encountered the comparisons of neurons in our brains and cosmic entities. Probably the numbers are no longer considered scientifically valid. I was thinking of Cleopatra's meeting death like a lover, and also of Hamlet's *What a piece of work is . . . man! how noble in reason! how infinite in faculty! in form and moving how express and admirable! in action how like an angel! in apprehension how like a god! the beauty of the world! the paragon of animals! And yet, to me, what is this quintessence of dust?* —Hamlet 2.ii. And Emily Dickinson's brain which is wider than the sky, deeper than the sea, and just the weight of God. What is lost when individual beings die, their brains packed with all those entanglements? Perhaps nothing is really lost? Oh, I see that this question has two conflicting meanings.

ACKNOWLEDGMENTS

Some of these poems have appeared in the following journals, some in earlier versions or with different titles:

Boulevard: THE PARABLE OF THE UMBRELLA THORN TREE

Canary: LATE WINTER IN PLAGUE TIME

Image: THE OLD WOMAN READS ECCLESIASTES AND THE SONG OF SONGS

LIBER: A Feminist Review, fall 2022: TACHYCARDIA (AGAIN) (early version); RITUAL IN PLAGUE TIME (early version); MOTHER/DAUGHTER DREAM; PHOTO OF A YOUNG WOMAN

Lilith: SUMMER

New Letters: I CANNOT DO THIS IN PROSE; TIME; SLOWLY [*He goes down…*]; SLOWLY [*The image of a man…*]; WE ALL KNOW; WHAT THEY SAY, SLOWLY THEY SAY, THEY SAY

Smartish Pace: TACHYCARDIA (AGAIN)

Tablet: TIME [*Time goes by…*]; RITUAL IN PLAGUE TIME I; RITUAL IN PLAGUE TIME II; SUMMER (excerpt), and ELUL (excerpt)

The Arkansas International: ANYTHING IN MOTION; NOCTURNE; GOLDBERG VARIATIONS IN DOUBLE-PLAGUE TIME

The Atlantic, March 2022: KEEPING THE DRAGON

The Georgia Review: LATE AUTUMN GINKOS; SOLITUDE

The Nation: ORACLE: AFTER; EVENING IN PLAGUE TIME

Tikkun: PRAYER

Deep gratitude to the women in my online poetry group, especially Ann Fisher-Wirth, Penelope Scambly Schott, Louisa Howerow, and Wendy Carlisle, for inspiration, encouragement, and wise critique; to my Drew students for sharing their courage; to Rebecca Gayle Howell, Judith Vollmer, Joan Larkin, Ellen Doré Watson, Tess O'Dwyer, Martha Nell Smith, Don Yorty, Richard Tayson and Peter Pitzele, for helping me to keep breathing as a poet.

RECENT TITLES FROM ALICE JAMES BOOKS

Wish Ave, Alessandra Lynch

Autobiomythography of, Ayokunle Falomo

Old Stranger: Poems, Joan Larkin

I Don't Want To Be Understood, Joshua Jennifer Espinoza

Canandaigua, Donald Revell

In the Days That Followed, Kevin Goodan

Light Me Down: The New & Collected Poems of Jean Valentine,
   Jean Valentine

Song of My Softening, Omotara James

Theophanies, Sarah Ghazal Ali

Orders of Service, Willie Lee Kinard III

The Dead Peasant's Handbook, Brian Turner

The Goodbye World Poem, Brian Turner

The Wild Delight of Wild Things, Brian Turner

I Am the Most Dangerous Thing, Candace Williams

Burning Like Her Own Planet, Vandana Khanna

Standing in the Forest of Being Alive, Katie Farris

Feast, Ina Cariño

Decade of the Brain: Poems, Janine Joseph

American Treasure, Jill McDonough

We Borrowed Gentleness, J. Estanislao Lopez

Brother Sleep, Aldo Amparán

Sugar Work, Katie Marya

Museum of Objects Burned by the Souls in Purgatory, Jeffrey
   Thomson

Constellation Route, Matthew Olzmann

How to Not Be Afraid of Everything, Jane Wong

Brocken Spectre, Jacques J. Rancourt

No Ruined Stone, Shara McCallum

ALICE JAMES BOOKS is committed to publishing books that matter. The press was founded in 1973 in Boston, Massachusetts to give women access to publishing. As a cooperative, authors performed the day-to-day undertakings of the press. The press continues to expand and grow from its formative roots, guided by its founding values of access, excellence, inclusivity, and collaboration in publishing. Its mission is to publish books that matter and preserve a place of belonging for poets who inspire us. AJB seeks to broaden our collective interpretation of what constitutes the American poetic voice and is dedicated to helping its artists achieve purposeful engagement with broad audiences and communities nationwide. The press was named for Alice James, sister to William and Henry, whose extraordinary gift for writing went unrecognized during her lifetime.

Designed by Alban Fischer

Printed by Versa Press